D1570237

Christmas Greeting

To

From

A Merry Christmas

MERRY CHRISTMAS

A Merry Christmas

To:

From:

Be Merry
& Bright

Season's
Greetings

Noel

Joy

HOLLY JOLLY

FROM SANTA

HO·HO·HO

JOY TO THE WORLD

TO

FROM

Have a Merry Christmas

TO FROM TO FROM TO FROM

HOPE ☀ LOVE ☀ JOY HOPE ☀ LOVE ☀ JOY HOPE ☀ LOVE ☀ JOY

To

From

Peace

To

From

To

From

TO :

FROM :

TO

FROM

TO

FROM

TO :

FROM :

TO :

FROM :

TO

FROM

Merry Christmas.

A Bright Christmas

To _____ From _____

To

From

Merry Christmas

MERRY CHRISTMAS MERRY CHRISTMAS MERRY CHRISTMAS MERRY CHRISTMAS

HAPPY HOLIDAYS HAPPY HOLIDAYS HAPPY HOLIDAYS HAPPY HOLIDAYS

PEACE HOPE LOVE PEACE HOPE LOVE PEACE HOPE LOVE PEACE HOPE LOVE

To

From

To

From

To

From

SOY CANDLE
· HANDMADE ·

A. MERRY. CHRISTMAS, AND HAPPY NEW-YEAR

A merry Christmas

Christmas Greetings

Christmas

A very happy Christmas

Kindest Greetings for Christmas

eat
drink
and be
merry

warm
winter
wishes

LET IT SNOW

hot cocoa
&
sweaters

Fond Christmas Greetings!

TO

FROM

To
FROM

To
FROM

To
FROM

To
FROM

To
FROM

joy

Wishing you a Merry Christmas

Merry Christmas

Warm Wishes

With Love

Happy Holidays

For You

With Love

Let it Snow!

Fa la la la la

TO DO

TO DO

WISH LIST · PARTY

TO DO

TO DO

PARTY · WISH LIST

TO DO

WISH LIST

PARTY

TO DO

TO DO

To

From

To

From

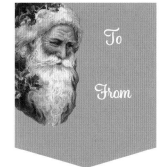
To

From

To

From

CHRISTMAS WISHES   SILENT NIGHT

Christmas Greetings

A Happy Christmas

A happy Christmas

A JOYFUL CHRISTMAS
over

To

From

To

From

To

From

Merry
and
Bright

To
From

To
From

To
From

To
From

To
From

To
From

To

FROM

To

FROM

JOY!

MERRY
CHRISTMAS

· PEACE ON EARTH ·

SEASON'S
GREETINGS

NOEL

To

FROM

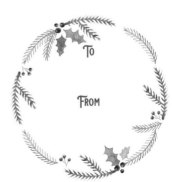

To

FROM

NOEL

To
From

To
From

To

From

peace on earth   *joy to the world*   *peace hope love*

HAVE A
JOLLY ♡ HOLIDAY

It's the most wonderful time of the year

Merry and **Bright**

Let it **Snow**

MERRY
CHRISTMAS
to you

SEASON'S
GREETINGS

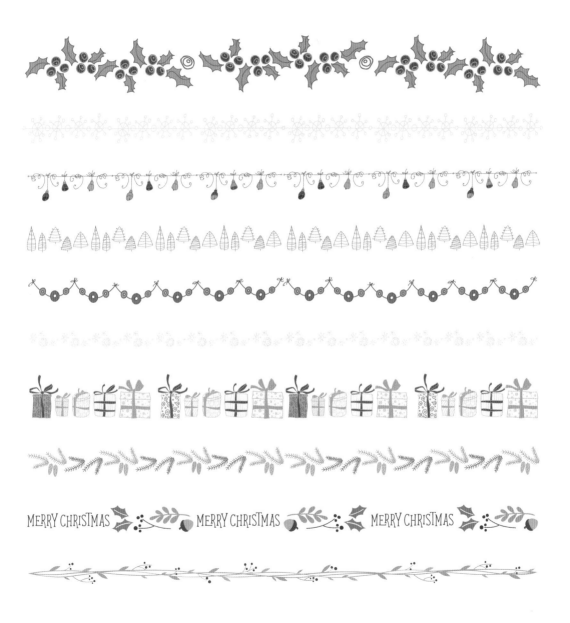

MERRY CHRISTMAS   MERRY CHRISTMAS   MERRY CHRISTMAS

HAVE A HOLLY JOLLY CHRISTMAS

HO-HO-HO

Believe IN THE Magic OF Christmas

Joyful

MERRY Christmas

Season's Greetings

MERRY CHRISTMAS

NOËL

Happy Holidays

SEASON'S GREETINGS

DEAR
SANTA

HO
HO
HO

To

From

To

From

To

From

To

From

PEACE ON EARTH

Christmas PARTY

Christmas PARTY

Christmas PARTY

Christmas PARTY

Christmas PARTY

Christmas PARTY

May your days be Merry & bright

SHOPPING	WISH LIST
SHOPPING	WISH LIST
SHOPPING	SEE SANTA
SHOPPING	DECORATE
SHOPPING	MAIL CARDS
SHOPPING	MAIL GIFTS

it's the MOST WONDERFUL time of the Year

Be jolly

peace love & joy

JOY

warm WISHES

happy HOLIDAYS

Joyeux Noël

Merry Christmas

Believe in the Magic of Christmas

MERRY CHRISTMAS!

MERRY CHRISTMAS TO YOU
SANTA CLAUS POST OFFICE
HAPPY HOLIDAYS
APPROVED
Merry Christmas
R NORTH POLE
№ 386

MERRY CHRISTMAS TO YOU
SANTA CLAUS POST OFFICE
HAPPY HOLIDAYS
APPROVED
Merry Christmas
R NORTH POLE
№ 386

HAPPY HOLIDAYS!

Christmas Greetings

Party!

Party!

Party!

To Do!
be
Merry &
Bright

To Do!

To Do!

Gifts

Gifts

TO

FROM

TO

FROM

TO

FROM

TO

FROM

WISHING YOU A VERY MERRY

CHRISTMAS

MERRY CHRISTMAS

AND HAPPY NEW YEAR

HAVE A VERY
MERRY
CHRISTMAS
&
HAPPY NEW YEAR

MERRY CHRISTMAS

AND HAPPY NEW YEAR

WE WISH YOU A MERRY

CHRISTMAS

AND HAPPY NEW YEAR

WISH YOU A MERRY

CHRISTMAS

&
HAPPY NEW YEAR

MERRY CHRISTMAS

AND HAPPY NEW YEAR

WE WISH YOU A MERRY

CHRISTMAS

HAPPY NEW YEAR

HAVE A VERY
MERRY   MERRY
CHRISTMAS

To

From

To

From

Peace
on
Earth

To

From

Magic moments

HOLLY JOLLY

HAPPY HOLIDAYS

merry Christmas

Merry and Bright

LET it SNOW

DREAMS

Dear Santa!

SANTA POST

COME TRUE

GOOD TIDINGS TO YOU

Merry Christmas

To

From